The Little Book of Free and Found

by Julie
Illustrations I

LITTLE BOOKS WITH BIG IDEAS

Published 2013 by Featherstone Education, an imprint of Bloomsbury Publishing Plc
50 Bedford Square, London, WC1B 3DP
www.bloomsbury.com

ISBN 978-1-4729-0409-6

Text © Julie Mountain 2013
Illustrations © Mike Phillips
Cover photographs © Julie Mountain

Printed and bound in India by Replika Press Pvt. Ltd.

1 3 5 7 9 10 8 6 4 2

This book is produced using paper that is made from wood grown in managed, sustainable forests. It is natural, renewable and recyclable. The logging and manufacturing process conform to the environmental regulations of the country of origin.

**To see our full range of titles
visit www.bloomsbury.com**

Contents

Introduction

Early years practitioners are known to be resourceful and creative, and these qualities are even more valuable as budgets become tighter. Luckily, a wealth of low-cost or no-cost play resources are close at hand, and this book sets out to provide practitioners with guidance on choosing free and found resources, risk-assessing their use, and encouraging children's creative use of the objects in their free and found collection. 'The Little Book of Free and Found' gives practitioners the knowledge and confidence to enrich the curriculum by 'wombling': collecting and using materials that other people no longer have a use for! This Little Book will invigorate outdoor play with unusual and unique resources that harness children's innate desire to experiment. Low-cost and no-cost resources offer phenomenal 'play value' and can meet the challenge of providing children with adventurous, challenging outdoor play.

The special nature of outdoor play

Outdoors is of course so different to indoors and offers children experiences that simply cannot be provided elsewhere. In the outdoor play space, activity is influenced not just by the resources available, or by children's own fascinations or practitioners' objectives, but by an array of endlessly varying factors: the weather, ambient noise and the temperature, views in and out of the site, the season and the time of day to name just a few. A flexible and dynamic outdoors, rich in tantalising stimuli, will make the most of the distinctive and special nature of the outdoors. Children who are unable to play outdoors regularly and for sustained lengths of time are significantly deprived.

Indoor and outdoor provision should be complementary and should be available simultaneously, allowing children to make informed choices about where they want to take their play. Many children will choose to be outdoors, where they can move freely, be noisy, collaborate, communicate and be expansive in the way they execute their ideas. Equally, they may choose to while away their time looking at books, pottering around plants or daydreaming. Outdoors, children are able to extend and take charge of their play; generosity of time outdoors and the ability to move freely between indoors and out are essential to children's sustained and shared thinking.

What are free and found resources?

Children are naturally curious and are risk-takers by habit and inclination. They tinker and mould. They question and test. They construct and deconstruct. Play resources should nurture and not limit children's imagination and creativity, and it is becoming clear that open-ended objects, provided in abundance, offer better 'play value' than expensive, fixed play features.

In this book, the phrase 'free and found resources' describes objects that can be used within children's play, but which are not necessarily designed for that purpose. It includes:

▶ Items donated by others – parents, local businesses (e.g. crates, containers)

▶ Items salvaged or scavenged that would otherwise go to waste (e.g. tyres, fabric offcuts)

▶ Low-cost items with high play value (e.g. from charity shops, car boot sales or scrap stores).

Free and found natural materials are compelling and are crucial in helping children reconnect with nature. Man-made free and found objects are also fascinating and provide insight into how our world works. The engineers and artists of the future will find much to explore in an old mobile telephone, a crate of bottles or the innards of a piano.

These kinds of resources are not 'toys' in the traditional or legislative sense of the word and are unlikely to have been subject to the exhaustive safety tests applicable to commercially available toys. This means that you will need to take a common sense approach to the collection, use and storage of your free and found resources; page 13 offers advice on this.

Affordances

An 'affordance' is something in the environment that offers opportunities for action or exploration; something that provides or 'affords' a function.

The most important factor in the provision of high quality outdoor play is not, however, the environment or the resources in it: knowledgeable and enthusiastic adults are crucial to unlocking the potential of outdoors.*

Practitioners who value and understand the potential of outdoors and who are confident in leading learning outdoors will have the necessary skills to make the most of the resources and the space available. Outdoor play has marked and positive effects on children's wellbeing; adults who are sensitive to children's cultural and emotional needs will be able to harness the special nature of outdoor play to meet these needs. A successful outdoor practitioner:

► Has a clear understanding of each child's needs and undertakes observations as rigorously outdoors as indoors

► Encourages risk taking in children and in their own practice

► Has appropriate clothing and footwear for the weather and the activity

► Models positive behaviours outdoors; encourages children's independence and problem solving abilities

► Records and evaluates the use of outdoor resources and shares what they know with parents and fellow practitioners.

* from the Shared Vision and Values for Outdoor Play in the Early Years – see 'Further research and useful websites', page 60.

The early years curriculum

Free and found resources have a meaningful role to play in the delivery of your early years curriculum; inventing new uses for unusual or familiar objects will stimulate your own creativity as a practitioner as well as that of your children. A rich and rewarding early years curriculum encompasses not just early learning goals – which can change – but also addresses many of children's fundamental needs: to feel valued, to experience joy and exhilaration, to understand the value of perseverance, to name just three.

The activities in this Little Book bring together the early learning goals from each of the Prime and Specific Areas of Learning and are chosen to ensure they support the overarching principles of the EYFS. In particular, children's communication and language skills are grown through these activities. Each activity requires respectful listening (to adults and other children), careful attention to detail and will stimulate increasingly sophisticated questions and language use.

As you work through the activities, you may well find curriculum connections that meet your children's particular needs; the table on page 7 offers just a snapshot of how you could use this book to support children's progress towards the EYFS early learning goals.

Early Learning Goal	Key 'free and found' activities
Communication and language	
Listening and attention	Well dressings; Geocaching treasure hunt; Mini farm
Understanding	Grass paintings; Junk deconstructors; Stick bread
Speaking	Create your own den kit; Ice pendants; Bottle babies
Physical development	
Moving and handling	Parkour; Frost/mud writing; Create your own den kit
Health and self-care	Take a line for a walk; Alternative allotments; Junk constructors
Personal, social and emotional development	
Self-confidence and self-awareness	Stick bread; Mini farm; Parkour
Managing feelings and behaviour	Junk deconstructors; Green man clay faces; Story makers
Making relationships	Create your own Den kit; Bottle babies; Stick skills
Literacy	
Reading	Story makers; Take a line for a walk; Geocaching
Writing	Frost/mud writing; Stick skills; Nature's paint palette
Mathematics	
Numbers	Geocaching; Stick skills; Create your own den kit
Shape, space and measures	Junk constructors; Junk deconstructors; Grass paintings
Understanding the world	
People and communities	Green man clay faces; Well dressings; Stick skills
The world	A Micro-pond; Water, water, everywhere; Ice pendants
Technology	Alternative allotments; Junk deconstructors; Stick bread
Expressive arts and design	
Exploring and using media and materials	Ice pendants; Stick flags; Nature's paint palette
Being imaginative	Grass paintings; Well dressings; Junk constructors

Sourcing and managing free and found resources

The beauty of free and found treasure is most definitely 'in the eye of the beholder' – one person's junk being another person's valued play resource! Each of the suggested activities in the book includes an inventory, but it will be helpful to start a 'wanted' list, to include some or all of the items listed below. Post this on the staffroom wall, parents' notice board or even on your favourite social networking site to recruit others to your 'free and found' sourcing campaign.

▶ Food and drink crates
▶ Cardboard tubes
▶ Fabric samples and offcuts; balls of wool; carpet tiles
▶ Sheets
▶ Fruit and veg (not all free and found resources have to be long-lived!)
▶ Hay or straw
▶ Sand, sawdust
▶ Timber offcuts; log slices; tree trunks; woodchips
▶ Tarpaulins and tents, reflective blankets
▶ Plant pots (plastic or terracotta)
▶ Broken items children can tinker with or 'repair' – e.g. small appliances
▶ Bricks, pavers and blocks
▶ Old (but still usable) tools
▶ Gutters and pipes, buckets, dishes and containers
▶ One-litre and two-litre drinks bottles and bottle tops
▶ Corks; conkers; fir cones; leaves
▶ Sticks and canes
▶ Sheep fleece or wool
▶ Tyres and tubes

The concepts of 'generosity' and 'abundance' are key to the provision of high quality outdoor play experiences and refer to more than just physical quantities of materials, although this is important. The richness and variety of children's play is enhanced when they have an abundance of time and space in which to experiment. Playful adults, prepared to take time to support and extend children's play but who know when to stand back and allow children to lead their own learning, are crucial.

Aim to plan your outdoor space so that wherever possible, children are able to return to a scenario to shape it and explore the materials further. This means that storage should be abundant and generously proportioned to allow equipment to be easily accessed. Whilst clearing up is an important part of any child's daily routine, it shouldn't be allowed to interrupt play unnecessarily, particularly if children are deeply engaged in play.

Free and found treasure troves

Never walk past a skip without peering into it! Free and found resources are everywhere and collecting them requires only a keen eye for 'affordances' and the confidence to ask a stranger to give you something for nothing. When you find an interesting and reliable source, keep going back to it and build relationships with regular suppliers – perhaps by sending a photo of children making creative use of the donated items or by inviting donors to see for themselves how their contributions are being used.

Wherever possible, always ask permission before scavenging an item, whether it's from a skip or a tip, a shop or a park. Householders and builders are often very generous but do appreciate being asked before items are acquired from their skips. Emailing or writing to potential suppliers can be profitable; consider asking them to meet you to discuss what you might be able to have and how the donation will benefit the children you work with.

When sourcing natural materials, observe the Countryside Code and do not pick anything that's still growing, or dig for anything (e.g. chalk or clay) unless you have permission to do so.

Hunt for 'found' treasure in:

▶ Supermarket, DIY and homeware stores' delivery bays – for huge cardboard boxes, plastic crates, bubble wrap, etc.

▶ Carpet and fabric suppliers – for the inner tubes of fabric bolts and carpet rolls as well as for samples and offcuts.

▶ Builders' merchants and building sites – for materials, packaging, and timber offcuts.

- ▶ Parks and countryside areas – for natural materials such as leaves, conkers and chalk.
- ▶ Skips and tips – become an expert skip scavenger!

Seek 'free' treasure by:

- ▶ Contacting local businesses and membership organisations (e.g. Rotary).
- ▶ Borrowing resources – this works particularly well for very large items.
- ▶ Signing up to Freecycle, Freegle, Gumtree or one of the many local online communities set up to support recycling and reuse of unwanted items.
- ▶ Talking to farmers, allotment holders and plant nurseries – great for edible freebies, interesting visits and waste or excess items that you can 'repurpose'.
- ▶ Identifying and visiting local timber merchants, tree surgeons, stone suppliers and quarries – be ambitious: ask if you can have a huge rock, or a tree trunk.
- ▶ Becoming friends with the staff at your local tip and making regular visits.

Spend a tiny budget at:

- ▶ Pound stores and charity shops
- ▶ Jumble, table top and car boot sales
- ▶ Market stalls and the local tip's sale table
- ▶ eBay and online auction sites (search for 'collection only' items as these often go for pennies)
- ▶ Your nearest Scrapstore – there is usually a very reasonable joining fee, after which bags of treasure are free or at a nominal cost.

Making the first contact with a potential supplier is often the trickiest stage; the fear of a 'no' often prevents us from asking. However, a 'no' at the first time of asking might actually mean, 'not now', so remember to thank potential suppliers for their reply and say you'll get in touch in a few months' time to see if the situation has changed. This is also a good way of alerting possible suppliers to the fact that you are seeking something in particular (for example, a tree trunk or a broken appliance) and are prepared to wait a while!

Caring for your free and found resources

Before you acquire any items, you will need to consider storage, maintenance and replenishment of your collection. A small 'toolkit' will help to keep free and found resources in playable condition.

Maintenance toolkit: sharp adult scissors, roll of wide duct tape, double sided tape, string, antibacterial wipes, Phillips and flat screwdrivers, various sizes of cable ties, superglue.

Storage

▶ Storage of your new resources will depend on their size, purpose and weather resistance. You may feel that some items should only be accessed by adults; but consider carefully which items these will be. There is no reason why heavy or awkward items shouldn't be available to children; manoeuvring them could help with agility and collaboration.

▶ Consider storing your free and found objects outdoors in places where there is room for them to be fully explored in the context of other more established play resources.

Maintenance

▶ If it isn't possible to repair damaged items, you should discard the item and seek a replacement if possible. Look for:

  ▷ Damaged or sharp edges or surfaces that could cause cuts or grazes

  ▷ Discolouring or water damage: unattractive items may be ignored by children and will not therefore provide the compelling play experiences you seek to offer

  ▷ Poorly fitting connections or unintentional loose parts (i.e. through repeated use) can create finger traps

  ▷ Loose wires, fraying string or rope: these pose a strangulation or snapping risk. The use of rope, string and wire should always be supervised and these items must be put away beyond the reach of children at the end of a play session.

Replenishment

▶ The 'shelf life' of free and found resources will vary depending on the materials they are manufactured from, how they are being used and where they are stored. You should plan for regular replenishment of these resources.

▶ It won't always be possible to replace like with like; if you find that a particular resource is very popular with children, consider making an arrangement with a supplier to provide regular replacements.

▶ Regularly review how free and found resources are being used; where items are proving popular, consider increasing the quantity. Before deciding to remove less popular objects, try moving them to a different part of the play space, or combining them with other play resources to gauge whether a change of context adds value.

▶ Be generous: keep stocks of free and found resources high, so that the opportunities for exploratory and imaginative play are maximised – abundance will also enable children to play collaboratively and to sustain play for longer periods of time.

Health and safety of free and found resources

Attitudes to risk have evolved in recent years, with many adults questioning whether a health and safety culture that aims to protect children from harm is in fact preventing them from learning to manage everyday life experiences. A risk-free childhood is likely to lead to timid or indeed reckless children, unable to cope with the consequences of their own decision-making. Adventure and excitement are integral to a childhood rich in high quality outdoor play experiences – and adventure and excitement come with risk, danger and challenge 'built in'. Children's play should be 'as safe as necessary' and a common sense approach to risk assessment will facilitate this.

Children are instinctive risk-takers, right from birth; outdoor play satisfies the need for adventure and new experiences. The challenges children seek are not simply physical; outdoor play also encompasses intellectual and emotional risk-taking, and children's cultural background will also inform their willingness to test their own boundaries.

Adventurous, exciting play, with compelling and stimulating resources in a managed environment and with caring adults on hand to support the risk-taking, helps children encounter 'real life' risks with confidence.

Risk benefit analysis

Risk benefit analysis is a risk assessment tool for enabling high quality, exciting outdoor play, rather than preventing it. Supported by RoSPA and the Health and Safety Executive (see page 60 for contact details), a 'risk benefit' approach to risk assessment is now advocated by many local authorities and play providers. This means weighing the likelihood and severity of potential risks against the benefits and rewards of the activity and making a judgement based upon that understanding.

Many play activities come with intrinsic risks: climbing a tree, roller skating, digging in mud. However, it's clear that the benefits of these activities outweigh the risk of serious, life-changing injuries and so children continue to fall out of trees, graze knees and elbows and eat mud, just as generations have done before them. Risk cannot (and should not) be eliminated from children's play experiences; the trick is to ensure that the risk of life-changing injury is minimised and that the benefits significantly outweigh the risks.

Risk assessing free and found resources

Free and found resources are not usually 'real' play resources, and therefore they will not be tested to European or British safety standards as playthings. This should not preclude their use in children's play; it just means you have to be robust in your initial risk assessment and clear about how these resources will be managed and cared for.

Your risk benefits assessment should include:

▶ Description of the activity/resource

▶ Details of how children will benefit from participating in the activity or using the resource

▶ The possible hazards

▶ The likelihood of each hazard occurring and its severity

▶ Who could be exposed to the risk?

▶ The precautions in place to mitigate the risk

▶ Overall risk rating – i.e. do the benefits outweigh the risks?

There are several perceived barriers to the use of free and found resources; fear of injury is just one. Concerns about mess, storage, clearing up and the impression visitors or parents might get all prevent the creative re-use of free and found objects. Two strategies will help to alleviate these concerns:

Zoning

▶ Zone the play space into areas that lend themselves to particular types of play – for example, construction play; quiet contemplative play; messy/muddy play etc. If you use schema or an Early Excellence approach in your setting, you could plan your outdoor zones along similar lines.

▶ Zones can overlap (and should, in order to encourage free-flowing play experiences), but this approach will help to contain activities and the associated resources into places that can cope with them. It will reduce the likelihood of resources spreading across the whole site or interrupting other children's play.

▶ Where particular resources are confined to zones, mess is more manageable, and supervision easier. Accessible storage within each zone will allow children to take responsibility for clearing up – if the space must be cleared – at the end of the session.

Communication

▶ Share information with parents and other staff; take lots of photographs and record children's experiences and comments. Explain the benefits of the free and found resources you have, focusing on improving outcomes for children.

▶ Provide details of the risk benefit approach to risk assessment; this will help others feel confident about the use of free and found resources.

▶ Invite parents to participate in a 'free and found' outdoor play session; ask them to help you source new free and found resources. If parents understand the value of outdoor play with these resources they are more likely to support it in the future.

Grass paintings

Grass is green because the pigment in it, chlorophyll, reflects the green light in sunlight. The sunlight triggers a chemical reaction called photosynthesis and this produces food to allow the grass to grow. If access to light is restricted, grass changes colour and won't grow; when the light is returned, it will go green and start to grow again.

This simple experimental technique can be used to make temporary pictures in your grass. It works best and fastest in the summer but will work all year round – except in the snow!

Key skills:

understanding the natural world; creative expression; enquiring mind

What you need:

▶ A patch of grass – of any size

▶ Objects to cover the grass, for example: plastic bin bags; plates; rope; cardboard

▶ Weights, for example: hollow blocks, rocks or sticks

▶ Camera

What you do:

▶ Introduce this concept by covering a patch of grass with a solid, opaque object – such as a plastic plate or piece of cardboard. Weigh the object down so that sunlight is completely restricted.

▶ Leave the grass covered for a week, then uncover it and inspect the grass below. What colour is the grass? Why has it changed colour? How long does it take the grass to go green again?

▶ Encourage children to talk about the environmental conditions they altered: "we covered the grass"; "we hid the grass from the sun"; "no rain could get to this bit of grass".

▶ Once you've tested the technique, experiment on a larger scale, using a range of objects to make pictures in the grass. Thick ropes make good 'picture frames' and shapes cut from cardboard or black PVC bin bags can be used to create patterns in the grass.

▶ Picture ideas: a giant sunflower; a chequer board or hopscotch; a labyrinth; funny faces (labyrinths and hopscotch patterns can be used for play, until they recolour and disappear).

Staying safe:
There are no significant risk issues with this activity.

Other ideas...

▶ Create a photo diary of the project: each day, ask children to briefly lift the covering to photograph the grass below, and continue to do so once the coverings have been removed. Over a period of time you will gather a journal showing how sunlight affects the colour of grass.

▶ Collect green paint sample cards (free from DIY stores) and ask children to match the colours on them with the colour of the grass each day. Paint colours generally have a name as well as a number; ask children to think of names for the colours in your grass photographs.

▶ Use the photographs of the different shades of green and yellow to inspire paint colour mixing and Impressionist paintings.

Internet search:
Labyrinth pattern (search for images); photosynthesis for children

Ice pendants

Decorating trees in wintertime has been a traditional activity for generations. Ice pendants can be filled with natural or man-made materials and are fascinating to make, hang and watch melt!

Key skills:

understanding the natural world; creative expression

What you need:

▶ Containers, such as lids from margarine or ice cream tubs, shallow dishes or baking trays – these should be between 1cm and 3cm deep

▶ Water

▶ A collection of decorative objects – natural (e.g. berries, fruit slices, pine fronds, holly leaves) or man-made (e.g. tiny cogs, magnetic letters, glitter). You could ask a local florist if they have 'unsaleable' flowers you could use

▶ String or ribbon; scissors

▶ A very cold night (or a freezer!)

What you do:

▶ Identify a level place where the containers can stay undisturbed overnight.

▶ Fill each shallow container with water, and lay the decorative objects in the water. Don't cram the containers too full, otherwise there won't be enough frozen water to hold it all together. Less is more!

▶ Fold lengths of string in half and place the folded ends of one piece of string into each container. Ensure that plenty of the string is immersed in order to make a strong hanger for each pendant.

▶ Allow the containers to freeze overnight – it can sometimes take a day or two for them to freeze so make sure they are not in anybody's way. Once frozen, you may need to use a little warm water to ease the pendants out of their containers.

▶ Hang the frozen pendants from a tree or a washing line. Some of them should be hung low enough for children to explore using their senses. Depending on the daytime and overnight temperatures, and the size of the pendants, they should last a day or two.

▶ If, despite your best efforts, it just doesn't get cold enough outdoors to freeze your pendants, put them in the freezer overnight!

Staying safe:

Children should be able to participate in all parts of this activity; ensure children are appropriately clothed for outdoor play in freezing weather. Warm drinks afterwards will help!

Other ideas...

▶ Visit a local park or woodland to collect natural materials for the pendants; you could come back here later to hang them for the delight of other park users.

▶ Freeze water in an outdoor water tray or Tuffspot. Children will enjoy sliding objects across the ice, creating small world 'ice wonderlands' and of course breaking the ice up into tiny pieces.

Internet search:
ice decorations

A micro-pond

Ponds are amongst the most fascinating features any school or setting could create. Space and safety concerns are often barriers to creating a permanent pond, so this idea is about making use of your local community to introduce the concept in a small, shallow and temporary way. Hopefully, its success will inspire you to think about creating a permanent pond!

Key skills:
understanding the natural world; speaking and listening; enquiring mind

What you need:
▶ Pond type 1 requires a solid container – ask for donations or visit the tip to try and find an old 'Belfast' sink; an extra large, deep roasting tin; a plastic pond; or a large plant pot or trough

▶ Pond type 2 requires a length of scavenged butyl pond liner; short lengths of railway sleeper or heavy logs/timber; and pieces of carpet or carpet tiles

▶ A bucketful of water from an established pond, including pond weed

▶ Pond dipping equipment

What you do:

▶ Choose a quiet, sheltered space to locate your pond.

▶ To create pond type 1 simply fill your container with the 'borrowed' pond water, making sure there is some vegetation in there in order to provide food for pond herbivores.

▶ To create pond type 2, make a pond edge using the logs, railway sleepers or timber. Make a 'sandwich' of pond liner by placing the carpet or carpet tiles within the perimeter, laying the butyl liner over that, making sure the edges of the liner overlap the perimeter edging. Finish with another layer of carpet tiles within the edging – the carpet tiles protect the liner from punctures. After you have filled the pond, weigh down the overlapped liner with more logs.

▶ Top up the pond if necessary, ideally with water from a water butt or collected in a bucket, rather than from a tap. Encourage children to leave the pond alone for a week or so, to allow any creatures that arrived in the bucket of pond water to settle in.

▶ In order to allow creatures to enter and leave the pond, build 'steps' for them using bricks, rocks and logs inside the container, and on the outside.

▶ In springtime, it won't take long for your pond to become colonised. Frogs can travel up to half a kilometre from their 'base' in search of breeding sites so a shady, quiet, damp place outdoors will be very attractive.

Staying safe:

▶ Either pond type will be too small and too shallow for a child to fall into and be at risk. However, the pond itself and the creatures in it could be damaged so encourage children not to climb in!

▶ If you have any concerns, place netting or a piece of fence over the top of the pond and weigh it down.

▶ Wash hands with warm water and soap after pond dipping.

Other ideas...

▶ Use ID cards to help children identify pond creatures.

▶ Consider creating a permanent pond, or visiting a pond in a nearby school.

Internet search:
school pond ideas

Well dressings

Well dressings are beautiful paintings made from petals, leaves, moss and other natural materials, embedded into clay. Towns and villages in the English Peak District have been creating well dressings for hundreds of years, to celebrate the arrival of Spring and the purity of their natural springs and wells.

Key skills:
creative expression; hand-eye co-ordination; collaboration

What you need:

I will need

▶ Wooden picture frames, with a solid wooden backboard (you don't need the glass). The size will depend on the space you have, and the amount of time. A5 or A4 is a good size to start with.

▶ A shallow tray large enough to fit the frames' backboards in

▶ Clay (natural, or air drying), water in a spray bottle

▶ Rolling pin

▶ Sheets of paper the same size as the frames' apertures; pencils

▶ Flowers, leaves, moss, cones, beans, seeds etc.

What you do:

▶ Soak the frames' backboards overnight in water: this helps the clay to stick.

▶ Draw a well dressing design onto the paper, encouraging children to choose colours that can be matched using the natural materials collection.

▶ Score the backboard with a knife in a criss-cross pattern – this will help the clay stick to the frame.

▶ Fit the frame and its backboard together and fill the space where the picture would go with clay. Use a rolling pin to make sure the clay is smooth and level with the frame itself.

▶ Place the paper picture over the top of the clay, and use the point of the pencil to prick out the design's outline into the clay.

▶ Fill in the outline in the clay using natural materials. Outlines can be made using thin pieces of moss, sunflower seeds or bark, larger areas with overlapping petals or seeds pressed into the clay. It's a good idea to start from the middle and work outwards. Spray the clay with water to stop it from drying out too quickly.

▶ Locate your finished well dressing by the outdoor tap or water fountain; it will last for about a week or so, depending on the weather.

Staying safe:

▶ Children should be able to participate in all parts of this activity.
▶ Model the safe use of clay and the knife (for scoring).
▶ Wash hands thoroughly after the activity.

Other ideas...

▶ Use paper plates to make mini well dressings with very young children.

▶ In the Peak District, well dressings are community projects; why not ask a joiner to make a permanent frame for a well dressing, and involve parents and your local community in its creation each year?

Internet search:
well dressings

Green man clay faces

Green Men are traditional stone and wood carvings, often found at the top of columns and corbels in buildings. They are thought to celebrate pagan mythology and the faces usually appear to be masked entirely in leaves, seeds and petals.

Key skills:
creative expression; hand-eye co-ordination; enquiring mind

What you need:

▶ Pictures of Green Man faces – ideally, laminated for use outdoors

▶ Clay (natural or air-drying); clay carving tools

▶ Water spray bottle

▶ Flowers, leaves, moss, cones, beans, seeds, berries, etc.

▶ Trees or timber posts (e.g. fences, play equipment)

What you do:

▶ Show children the Green Man pictures and explain the mythological stories behind the carvings.

▶ Give each child a ball of clay about the size of their fist. Children should squash the clay onto a roughly textured tree trunk or wooden post – scoring the back of the clay using a twig can help it adhere more effectively.

▶ Use fingers or clay tools to mould the clay into a face shape, with eye sockets, a nose and a mouth and chin.

▶ Decorate the faces with the leaves and natural materials, creating hair, beards and moustaches, eyebrows and other crazy features. Spray with water whilst working the clay to keep it moist.

▶ Tour all of the Green Men, asking children about the materials they used and the personality of their Green Man. Remember to photograph each face, as it will only last for a few weeks before drying out.

Staying safe:

▶ Children should be able to participate in all parts of this activity.
▶ Wash hands after the activity and watch out for thorns on your found natural materials.

Other ideas...

▶ Look for Green Man carvings in your locality: they are likely to be in churches, on pub signs and in woodlands.

▶ Repeat the exercise, with children attempting to recreate their own faces as Green Men.

▶ Go out into the local park and create 'secret' Green Men – hidden faces on the trees that visitors will come across accidentally as they use the park.

Internet search:
Green Man myth

Create your own den kit

Den building kits are widely available from educational suppliers but can cost upwards of £150. For a fraction of this cost you can create your own bespoke kit, which will suit the age and ability of your children, and can be extended and replenished cost effectively over time. Many items can be scavenged from tips and skips, donated by parents or purchased in charity and pound shops, but what you include is entirely up to you and could change from week to week.

Den building appeals to children's desire to construct and create personalised spaces for themselves, as well as fostering imaginative and collaborative play. Therefore a den kit should contain items to encourage children to play in the den as well as build it – for example, binoculars (real or home-made), books, cuddly toys etc. from your existing play resources.

Key skills:
creative expression; collaboration; problem solving; gross motor skills; fine motor skills

What you need:

▶ A sturdy, lidded, waterproof box – it would be worth spending some money on this!

▶ Donations from parents: sheets; towels; blankets and duvet covers; net curtains; 'bags for life', etc.

▶ Found or scavenged objects: long sticks; timber planks; washing airer; shower curtain rings, etc.

► Donations from local businesses: carpet/cork tiles; clothes hangers; fabric bolt inner tubes, etc.
► 'Pound shopping': small tarpaulins; connectors (see below); tarpaulin pegs
► Connectors (these are the items that join the fabric and tarpaulins to structures – keep them together in a 'bag for life' within the den kit box): pegs; mini-karabiners; bag clips; bungee cords; string; rope washing line, etc.
► Make: flags

What you do:

► Children will enjoy freely exploring the contents of the den kit box and should be encouraged to test the materials and practice with the 'connectors' in different locations around your site.
► To enrich den play, consider adding themed items such as ropes and pulleys ('The Lighthouse Keeper's Lunch'), faux furs ('Where the Wild Things Are') or a tea set ('Alice in Wonderland').
► Use the features of your site to inspire different styles of den – for example, use play equipment, trees or a playhouse as the basic structure.

Staying safe:

► Check reclaimed materials or equipment for sharp edges – for example, sand the ends and edges of sticks and planks.
► Always pack ropes, string and bungees away in the den kit box after every play session.
► Wash linen items every few weeks and dry thoroughly to prolong their life.

Other ideas...

► Take your den kit to the park or woodland to extend the construction challenge for children.
► Develop fine motor skills by introducing new and more complex connectors, or by learning new knots. Pegs, or bungees with hooks on are simple ways to join fabric to a structure; karabiners require more dexterity and strength.

Internet search:
Den building; forest school dens

Stick flags

A stick collection is an important element of any outdoor play setting. Stick flags are easy to make and add colour and beauty to even the most unpromising stick.

Key skills:

hand-eye co-ordination; creative expression; agility

What you need:

▶ A book of fabric samples – ask a local fabric store or interior designer to donate these to you

▶ Patterned sheets or duvet covers – heavier fabrics work best

▶ Sewing machine and thread

▶ Sharp fabric scissors

▶ Sticks of various lengths and diameters

What you do:

▶ Fold squares or rectangles of fabric in half (seam sides together) so that the flag will be 'double sided'.

▶ You are going to sew around the edges of the folded fabric, leaving a narrow 'pocket' along one short edge, wide enough to allow a stick to be inserted. Don't worry about hems; the running stitch around the edges will prolong the life of the flag.

▶ Start sewing, using running stitch, in a corner opposite to the folded edge; sew up this edge towards the fold, then along the fold, then back down towards the long open edge, then along the long open edge.

▶ Don't sew all the way back to your starting point in the corner, but instead stop around 7 – 10cm before it, turn the fabric 90° and sew in a straight line back up to the top folded edge.

▶ You now have a double sided square or rectangle of fabric, with a pocket up one edge that should be wide enough for a stick.

Staying safe:

▶ The 'making' part of this project is not really for young children. Older children (e.g. 7+ years) could do the sewing, closely supervised by an adult.

▶ Ensure sharp nodes on the sticks are sanded smooth.

▶ Explain 'stick etiquette': sticks should be held and carried upright to prevent accidental pokes or trips.

Other ideas...

▶ Create pennants by using extra long lengths of fabric, and cutting a large V-shaped notch into one of the short ends.

▶ Make super quick stick flags by using double sided sticky tape to join the folded fabric together and create the 'pocket'. They won't last as long as sewn flags, but younger children can help make them.

▶ Personalise flags by printing your setting's logo onto special T-shirt inkjet paper and ironing it onto plain cotton flags.

▶ There are dozens of stick play ideas in 'The Stick Book' by Jo Schofield and Fiona Danks.

Internet search: —————————————
Playing with sticks

Story makers

Well-loved books tend to wear out quickly. Rather than throw them away because a page is damaged or missing, invent new stories by mixing and matching pages from several books. Books with few words work best for this idea.

Key skills:
speaking and listening; story telling; enquiring mind

What you need:

▶ A selection of old story books
▶ Laminating machine and laminating pouches
▶ Hole punch
▶ String/pegs/Blu-tack
▶ Lever arch binder or basket big enough to fit the laminated pages

What you do:

▶ Cut pages from the books, trimming each page to ensure it is smaller than A4 (or A3 if you are using an A3 laminator).

▶ Place the pages back-to-back and laminate, leaving a wide laminated margin, especially along the edge you intend to hole punch.

▶ Punch holes through the laminating plastic rather than the page itself. This will lengthen the life of each laminated page.

▶ Keep your new story pages in a basket or binder, with some string, Blu-tack and pegs.

▶ Encourage children to sift through the new story pages, describing what they think is happening on each page and organising the pages into new stories.

▶ Use the string, pegs and Blu-tack to attach pages to various features outdoors (or indoors) to create a story trail; think about how the context of each page could influence how children interpret the pictures and develop their play – for example, a page from 'Rapunzel' attached to the play equipment, a page from 'The Gruffalo' in the shrubbery, or 'Fix-It Duck' in the construction/mud pie area!

Staying safe:

▶ There are no significant risk issues with this activity.

Other ideas...

▶ Laminate pages from an entire book and ask children to retell the story in the correct order.

▶ Separate the text from the pictures, laminating them separately, and ask children to match the text to the pictures.

▶ Make secret boxes for children's treasure by cutting a chunk out of the pages (use a sharp craft knife to do this) but keeping the covers intact. You'll need a thick book to do this.

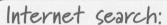

Internet search:

Check Pinterest for recycled book ideas

Geocaching treasure hunt

Geocaching is 21st century treasure hunting, with hidden 'caches' placed all around the world in urban and rural areas. In your setting it's a way of bringing new adventure to a treasure trail and can be as simple or as complex as you want it to be.

Key skills:
Problem solving; speaking and listening; collaboration

What you need:

▶ Small, waterproof containers for treasure: tiny jam jars; film canisters; small plastic food storage boxes; sweet boxes (e.g. TicTacs, Kinder)

▶ Treasure: this can be anything!

▶ A simple map or plan of your site

▶ Laminated clues

▶ Clipboards and pencils/chalkboard and chalk

What you do:

▶ Collect geocache containers and treasure from around the setting or ask parents to donate them.

- ▶ Make a very simple plan of your site, marking on the key features young children will recognise. You could also download an aerial view from the Internet.
- ▶ Choose hiding places for the caches. Ideal places will require children to search above and below their eye level and move items such as rocks, logs or branches.
- ▶ Place the treasure in the geocache containers and hide these around the garden or site.
- ▶ Create laminated clues for each cache. How you do this will depend on the age and ability of the children participating. It could be as simple as a photograph of the hiding place area or something connected to that place, for example a picture of a strawberry jam jar, with the cache hidden under leaves in your strawberry patch.
- ▶ More complex instructions might include a combination of directions, pictograms or cryptic clues, for example, a pictogram indicating a number of steps from a given point towards another given point. Six steps from the slide to the apple tree could be the number 6; then a picture of a foot; a picture of the slide; an arrow; then a picture of the apple tree.
- ▶ Children might like to use a clipboard and paper or a chalkboard to record their discoveries.

Staying safe:

- ▶ Carefully consider the geocache hiding places so that they offer appropriate challenge without encouraging children to incur unnecessary risk.

Other ideas...

- ▶ Ask each child to work with a parent or carer to collect a treasure item, place it in a tiny container, and hide it in the outdoor area to be happened upon during normal play outdoors.
- ▶ Weave stories into the caches, for example: write tiny fairy letters to place in the caches; theme each cache with something from a story.
- ▶ To encourage early map-reading skills, mark the locations onto your plan or aerial view, mark a very large chalk 'X' on the ground and mark it in the correct place on the plan too. Children should stand on top of the chalk X and seek the caches using just the information on their plan or aerial view.

Internet search:
Geocaching UK

Stick skills

Sticks remain one of the most popular play items for children of all ages. Their weight, texture, smell and shape are compelling and each is unique. An outdoor stick collection is an essential for any play-based setting and children will use their imagination to explore sticks' properties.

Key skills:
enquiring mind; hand-eye co-ordination; gross and fine motor skills; speaking and listening; creative expression

What you need:

▶ A generous stick collection: choose sticks of various lengths, diameters and textures, but avoid sticks with lots of nodes (where branches grew). Elder, hazel and willow make good play sticks.

▶ Bowsaw; loppers; secateurs

▶ Sandpaper

What you do:

▶ Simple maths: lay out sticks in a row from longest to shortest; narrowest to widest; make repeating patterns and shapes of various sizes; ask one child to make an irregular shape, and another child to copy it exactly or make a reflection of it (use a long stick to represent the 'mirror').

▶ Comparing and estimating: cut several long, straight narrow sticks into two 5cm sections, two 10cm long sections, one 20cm long section and one 50cm long section per stick. Mark each piece from each stick with coloured tape or paint/correction fluid so that you know they are part of the same set. Your sections make up a 1m length of stick – use them to discuss simple mathematical concepts such as 'how many...' and 'how long...' and to estimate the height or length of other features in the garden.

▶ Small world construction: cut sticks into various short lengths – minimum size around 2cm, maximum around 10cm. Choose sticks of different diameters and include some 'slices' of trunk or bigger branches. Store in a box or drawstring bag and use alongside other small world items to enrich play.

▶ Stick skeletons: examine the fossilised skeleton of a dinosaur; use your stick collection to recreate this skeleton full size, or to create your own imaginary dinosaur. Encourage children to think about the scale of a dinosaur – for example, compare the length of its leg bones to the children's. Chalk around the outline of your skeleton so that the dinosaur remains once the sticks are packed away. Children could also examine images of a human skeleton, and use the sticks to create their 'own' skeleton on the ground.

Staying safe:

▶ Cut sticks to size with the appropriate tools: secateurs for sticks up to 1cm in diameter, loppers for those up to 3cm in diameter and a bowsaw for larger sticks and logs.

▶ Sand the cut ends of sticks smooth, and chamfer the edges, to minimise the risk of splinters.

▶ Store sticks carefully when not in use – out of general reach might be sensible - and ensure that everyone carries them vertically when moving around the space, to avoid accidental pokes or trips.

Other ideas...

▶ Collect pebbles, cones, feathers, conkers and other natural materials to use for counting, pattern and shape exploration.

▶ 'The Stick Book' by Fiona Danks and Jo Schofield has dozens of clever ideas for using sticks.

Internet search:
children playing with sticks

Frost/mud writing

Make the most of pronounced seasonal changes and embrace the mess! Children adore playing in mud, and in snow and frost. A hard frost and an easily accessible set of short sticks can encourage even the most reluctant mark-makers to be the 'first person to ever write here!', and mud will always be a captivating prospect for children.

Key skills:
speaking and listening; fine motor skills, creative expression; understanding the natural world

What you need:

▶ A frosty day or a mud patch

▶ Sticks, and whittlers – vegetable peelers are ideal

▶ Camera

What you do:

▶ Identify the places around your site that succumb to hard frosts, so that you are ready to play on the first frosty day. North facing areas are more likely to stay frosty longer and morning frosts are usually the hardest.

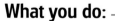

- ▶ Embrace the muddy patches outdoors, and enable children to make mud kitchens, splash in the mud and write with and in the mud.
- ▶ Choose sticks from your stick collection – for ergonomic mark-making they should be around 30cm long, and slightly thicker than a pencil.
- ▶ If you choose to, whittle the ends into a point so that children can make finer marks. Vegetable peelers are perfect 'first whittlers' for young children – or you could ask parents for donations. Build a collection of Y-shaped and 'Lancashire' style peelers to accommodate the different handgrip and whittling motion preferences individual children have.
- ▶ Mark-make in the frost; use the mud as the writing medium or the 'canvas'. Remember to photograph the marks as they won't last long!

Staying safe:

- ▶ Encourage safe whittling: children should always sit whilst whittling, and must whittle away from their bodies and towards the ground. A 'legs apart' or 'legs to one side' stance is safest.

Other ideas...

- ▶ Next time the freezer needs defrosting, pack the loose, soft ice tightly into a cool bag with a couple of freezer blocks. Use to create mini sculptures.
- ▶ Search for icicles – they also make excellent mark makers, so long as children can bear to hold them. Winter gloves are a must!
- ▶ Icicles can also be utilised to support measuring, sorting and estimating skills – use them to introduce simple timing and temperature concepts.
- ▶ Jump in icy puddles to smash up the surface – it's very cathartic!
- ▶ If you have a pond, you may be able to lift a more substantial piece of ice from its surface. Carefully drive a hole though the ice around 15cm from an edge (use a hand drill if you have one, or a Phillips screwdriver) and hang it from a tree or a canopy with strong string. Ensure the ice slab is at children's eye level and no higher; they will be able to examine the ice slab close-up.

Internet search:
playing with mud; playing with ice

Water, water everywhere

Playing with water is a crucial element of childhood, and lends itself to the decoding of mathematical concepts as well as a better understanding of the natural world. Outdoors is the perfect place for water play: expansive or complex ideas can be explored in confidence where there is no danger of slippery floors or damaged playthings.

Key skills:
enquiring mind; understanding the natural world; problem solving

What you need:

▶ Access to water; if you don't have an outdoor tap, have one installed – it will offer the best value of any investment in outdoor play!

▶ Large containers for water: an old sink, Tuff-spots, a tin bath, plastic trugs...

▶ Smaller vessels for pouring and splashing water: drinks bottles, spray bottles, sieves, jugs etc. All of these items can be found at your local tip, or ask parents to donate unwanted items

▶ A selection of dry natural materials: cones, conkers, feathers, pebbles, twigs and logs, etc.

What you do:

▶ Explore what happens to a pinecone when it gets wet. Try to collect a selection of cones from different tree species to compare shape, size and weight. Place a cone in the water, and leave one dry. Observe what happens. The pinecone 'closes' in order to protect the seeds inside from rain – dry seeds will blow further in the wind.

▶ Test what happens when water drops onto a duck or goose's feather, compared to a pigeon's feather. Drop one or two drops of water onto the feathers from the children's fingers – don't immerse them! The waterfowls' feathers are highly water repellent, in order to keep the bird warm and dry. Examine the feather with a magnifying glass and look at the way each section (barb) joins onto the others to create a watertight seal. What happens if you totally immerse the feathers? How long does it take to become soaked?

▶ Carefully punch small holes from the top to the bottom of a 1-litre bottle – use a screwdriver or the end of a sharp knife. Cover the holes with sticky tape, place the bottle in the water tray and fill it to the top with water. What happens when you remove the sticky tape? What do children notice about the way water escapes from the bottle? Water pressure at the bottom of the bottle is greater than at the top, so the water sprays further away, then this recedes as the water level drops.

▶ Challenge children's understanding of what floats and sinks, using a fairly deep container and a selection of scavenged objects, e.g. twigs, branches, leaves, cotton reels, pieces of fruit, marbles, ice, polystyrene. Ask children to hold each object and speculate as to whether it will float or sink. Compare objects of similar weight (e.g. a marble and an apple) and ask children to explain why one sinks and one floats.

Staying safe:

▶ Water play is very safe, but remember to dispose of water at the end of a play session, and turn outdoor taps off over holiday periods.

Other ideas...

▶ Use different sized vessels to compare water volumes, encouraging mathematical language such as bigger/smaller, faster/slower, deep/shallow, empty/full.

▶ Compare the ways water and sand flow through a funnel. What happens if you mix the sand and water?

Internet search:
early years water play

Nature's paint palette

Key skills:
fine motor skills; creative expression; speaking and listening; understanding the natural world

What you need:

▶ Containers for collecting and containers for crushing
▶ Wooden spoons, or mortar and pestle, short, or thick sticks – all for crushing with
▶ Paintbrushes
▶ Seive or tea strainer – optional
▶ Natural materials

What you do:

▶ Take a stroll to collect an abundance of berries and flower heads. If you are concerned about suitable berries, take an ID guide with you. Ideal berries and flowers include blackberries, elderberries, wild strawberries, sloes, damsons, buddleia, rose hips and grass.

- Discuss the colours you think each berry or flower will create when pounded – it may not be the colour children expect.
- Pound the berries and petals using thick sticks, wooden spoons or a mortar and pestle – encourage children to use full body movements to make a thick, sticky, pulpy mess. They could also squash the berries with their fingers or feet (use a shallow water tray). Some children find this difficult or unpleasant to do, whilst others will love the sensation.
- If you choose, sieve the pulp to separate the paint – however, children may enjoy painting with the pulp. Decant it into smaller containers so that children can take it around your outdoor space.
- Encourage children to mark make using the paint: think about hand prints, aboriginal-style dot and line marks, stick person figures on the tree trunks, or concentric circles in the sandpit.
- Edible berries can also be used as face or body paint – explore ideas around camouflage using mud or clay, crushed berries and earth toned clothing. Take photographs of children hiding with their camouflaged arms, legs and faces and share them at circle time, discussing how well the camouflages worked.

Staying safe:
- Use a plant ID guide if you are at all unsure about which species are safe to eat and which are poisonous.
- Wash hands thoroughly after the activity.

Other ideas...

- Crushed chalk, mixed with water to a thick paste, makes wonderful, long lasting white paint. Mark a trail of foot or handprints across the hard surfaces of your outdoor space. Mix with food colouring to make vivid shades.
- Make cordial using blackberries or elderflowers. Recipes are available online and it's very simple to do, with citric acid (natural preservative) cheaply and widely available in chemists.
- Make vegetable or fruit dyes and paints using the skin or peel of brightly coloured vegetables and the same pounding technique as the berry paints.

Internet search:
make berry paint; aboriginal art

Stick bread

Learning how to manage fire is a key skill for children, and cooking on a fire is a great way to enjoy and respect its power. Don't be put off by the apparent risks – campfires and cooking can be a regular feature in any setting.

Key skills:
speaking and listening; collaboration; understanding the natural world

What you need:

I will need

▶ Long sticks, approximately 2cm to 5cm in diameter and some short Y-shaped sticks to use as props

▶ Secateurs for cutting sticks to size, vegetable peelers for whittling

▶ Fire-making equipment (tinder, wood, matches) or a large disposable barbecue

▶ Fire safety equipment (bucket of water, fire blanket, heatproof gloves, first aid kit)

What you do:

▶ First build a fire, or light the barbecue. For safety reasons, choose a place you can separate from the rest of the play space. If you don't have a fire pit, build a fire in a metal container such as a large turkey roasting tin or use a large disposable barbecue, removing the metal grille. Lift the barbecue or tin off the ground using bricks.

▶ Allow the fire to get going whilst children make the dough. A simple unleavened bread recipe works well on an open fire and is great fun for children to mix: 500g plain flour, 1tsp baking powder, 2 tbsp sugar, 300 - 500ml water and a little oil. The dough needs to be firm enough to roll and wrap so adjust the water to suit.

- ▶ Roll the dough into thick worms around 10cm long and twirl them around the end of the sticks.
- ▶ Cook the dough over the coals of the fire, rather than the flames. Holding the sticks can be tiring for young arms, so using short Y-shaped sticks as props will help keep the dough in the correct position over the fire – children should hold the end of their stick in place.
- ▶ Check the bread is cooked by breaking a small piece off or by pressing the dough – it should yield slightly but spring back. Allow the bread to cool slightly before eating.

Staying safe:

- ▶ As a minimum, you must have a bucket of water close to the fire and a first aid kit containing burn gel and sterile eyewash, as well as the standard items. Ideally, have a fire blanket handy.
- ▶ Create a boundary around the fire, using logs or a rope. Explain to children that they may not step over the boundary.
- ▶ Light the fire with long safety matches, lighting the tinder first.
- ▶ Use long sticks – this will ensure children are an appropriate distance from the flames or embers but can still reach.
- ▶ Do not leave the fire unattended and ensure it is thoroughly extinguished at the end of the cooking session, using the bucket of water. Allow the embers and ash to cool before disposing of them.
- ▶ Wash hands thoroughly before preparing the dough and after cooking.

Other ideas...

- ▶ Marshmallows and cocktail sausages are also quick and simple to cook on a stick over a fire.
- ▶ Cook spoonfuls of pancake mix on a cast iron skillet or paella dish, over the hot embers of the fire.
- ▶ Make charcoal by slowly 'cooking' the stick itself in the coals of the fire. Allow to cool thoroughly before using it! The spent embers of wood also make good mark-makers.

Internet search:
children's campfire cooking

Alternative allotments

Key skills:
fine motor skills; understanding the natural world; enquiring mind

What you need:

▶ Scavenged or begged containers, for example: old wellington boots; Belfast sink; tin bath; chimney pot; wire or wicker shopping basket; Croc shoe; tin can; scallop shell; handbag; tyres; chest of drawers

▶ Compost; gravel or bark chips; pebbles or pieces of broken pot ('crocks')

▶ Child-sized gardening tools; screwdriver or drill

▶ Plants – ask for cuttings from parents or local allotment holders

▶ Paint and paintbrushes (optional)

What you do:

▶ If possible, punch or drill drainage holes in the bottom of the containers; if it's not possible, be sure to avoid over-watering – this can be a challenge with enthusiastic young gardeners.

▶ If you choose to, paint or decorate the containers – for example, painted tyres or old pots can really brighten up a garden. Don't plant into them until they are thoroughly dry.

▶ Place a thin layer of gravel in the base of each container – this aids drainage – then fill up with compost leaving around 5cm clear to the rim of the container. If the container is very small (e.g. scallop shell) it won't be possible to do this, but tiny containers lend themselves to succulents and rock plants, which can cope with drier conditions.

▶ Plant the cuttings or plants into the compost and add a thin layer of gravel or bark chippings to help retain moisture and prevent weeds. Water well.

▶ Place your alternative allotments in a sunny spot – perhaps all in one place to make a striking spectacle, or around the garden to provide amusing and colourful displays. Consider hanging the containers from fences or walls, as well as placing them on the ground.

▶ Remember to water containers regularly, especially in dry weather.

▶ Harvest ripe crops and cook or eat raw – remember the taste of cooked and raw vegetables is very different, and a fussy eater may choose to try vegetables or fruit they have grown themselves.

Staying safe:

▶ Gardening is a safe and enjoyable activity for children of all ages. Make it easier for children by providing appropriately-sized gardening tools – buy smaller versions of 'real' tools, not 'toy' tools. Real child-sized tools are properly proportioned and weighted for small hands and are designed for regular and frequent use.

▶ Wash hands thoroughly after the activity.

▶ Check larger planted areas for fox and cat faeces – a newly planted area can be very attractive!

Other ideas...

▶ Visit a local allotment – the committees are often very keen to encourage young gardeners and their families and should welcome your visit. Ask to taste ripe crops, and to harvest crops or collect seeds yourselves to take back for an allotment picnic.

▶ Ask families to donate sunflower seeds at the end of the flowering season; keep them dry and plant them indoors in spring, taking them outdoors as the weather improves.

Internet search:

unusual plant containers; gardening with children

Junk constructors

'Loose parts' are objects that are not fixed in a permanent location outdoors and frequently they are items that would not usually be considered as play resources. Play with 'loose parts' is open ended, flexible and child initiated. This kind of play affords children opportunities to experiment and take physical and intellectual risks that play with conventional play equipment does not. The key is abundance – be generous with loose parts and source multiple items wherever possible.

Key skills:

gross and fine motor skills; hand-eye co-ordination; creative expression; problem solving; speaking and listening; collaboration

What you need:

▶ Scrap and junk, for example: cardboard boxes, castors, wheels and axles, planks of wood; plastic conduit; tyres; pipe lagging; sheets and blankets; baskets; saucepans and bowls; crates

▶ Connectors: string; garden flexi-wire; masking tape; karabiners; elastic and elastic bands; Velcro ties, etc.

▶ Simple tools: child-sized screwdrivers and hammers; scissors – supervise their use closely

What you do:

▶ To start your loose parts collection, visit the tip, scavenge from skips and ask for donations.

▶ Establish a secure place to store loose parts – decide whether free access is appropriate, taking into consideration the age, agility and co-ordination of your children as well as the nature of the objects themselves.

▶ Support children to create structures and sculptures with their junk/loose parts. Use the connectors to join loose parts together – you may need to help children do this, but only intervene if really necessary as there are myriad opportunities to refine motor skills during this activity.

▶ The lifespan of children's creations are likely to be fleeting, so photograph them before taking them to pieces to re-use the loose parts. If possible, keep models intact for several days to allow children to return to their work over a period of time and adapt their ideas and challenge their thinking.

Staying safe:

▶ Scrap modelling is a risky activity but you can minimise risks by taking sensible precautions: ensure all items are clean, grease-free, smooth and in good condition. Avoid objects with obvious finger traps. Supervise and model the safe use of tools. Always put away string and ropes at the end of a session – and supervise their use during the session.

▶ Wash hands thoroughly after the activity.

Other ideas...

▶ Challenge children to make objects that move – using rollers, pipes, bottles, castors and wheels.

▶ Create a rocket or playhouse using huge cardboard boxes – usually available at the tip or at local businesses. Show children a clip of the astronomical film 'Secret of the Cardboard Rocket', and read the stories 'Crispin: The Pig Who Had It All' and 'Not a Box' (both about imaginary cardboard box adventures).

▶ Extend the play value of existing equipment such as climbing frames by using the loose parts in and around them – for example creating balancing beams, dens and shelters.

Internet search: ───────────────
outdoor junk modelling for children

Junk deconstructors

As all practitioners (and parents) know, children's intrinsic curiosity is often satisfied by taking things to pieces. Encourage them to question how common objects are constructed and speculate about what happens inside familiar items by deconstructing them.

Key skills:

gross and fine motor skills; hand-eye co-ordination; problem solving; enquiring mind

What you need:

▶ Unwanted household objects: simple items such as small chair or a fan and more complex items such as a DVD player or mobile phone

▶ DIY tools: screwdrivers and hammers (child sized); wire cutters and pliers. If you can borrow an electric screwdriver, children will enjoy the thrill of using it

▶ Tarpaulin

What you do:

▶ In a small group, examine the object you plan to deconstruct. What can children tell you about the materials it's made from, its size, how it's joined together, who might have made it, what it's used for, and what the pieces inside might look like?

▶ Draw pictures of the object – photograph the drawings and the object for 'before and after' pictures.

▶ Discuss and agree how to take the object to pieces, examining the way it's constructed and the tools you have available. Make sure you show children how to use the tools and give them the opportunity to practice the movements and precision required before they begin on the object itself.

▶ On a large tarpaulin, take the object apart, ensuring you keep all the pieces. If children don't know the names of each part as it is deconstructed (and they are unlikely to), discuss what the part does and make up descriptive names for each piece.

▶ Use the deconstructed pieces – see below.

Staying safe:

▶ Minimise risks by using appropriately-sized tools and choosing objects that can be taken to pieces without the need for specialist tools or adult strength.

▶ Loosen screws slightly before children attempt to remove them.

▶ When using tools, children should wear a protective 'rigger' glove on the hand not operating the tool. They may also enjoy wearing protective goggles, although these are unlikely to be needed from a safety perspective.

▶ Undertake these activities in small groups in order to offer children the close attention they will require.

Other ideas...

▶ Put the object that the children deconstructed back together. Use memory, drawings and photographs to recall what it looked like and in what order it was deconstructed.

▶ Use the parts of the deconstructed item to create something new (junk modelling on smaller scale).

▶ If you've deconstructed a small item (such as a mobile phone), use the pieces to inspire artworks by gluing them to a sheet of cardboard or making a mini-sculpture.

▶ Make an 'exploded' diagram of the object you deconstructed: a photograph of the item in the centre of a piece of paper, with the actual parts glued to the perimeter of the paper and string linking them to their location in the original object.

Internet search:
tinkering school; children taking things apart

Mini farm

Caring for living creatures brings out children's nurturing qualities, but keeping animals can be problematic. Overcome this, and gain all the benefits of living alongside an animal, by borrowing one for a day or a week at a time. Ask a parent or local smallholder to lend you an animal and to come in and talk to children about how to care for it.

Key skills:
collaboration; problem solving; understanding the natural world; speaking and listening

What you need:

▶ A borrowed animal!
▶ Housing for your animal(s) – borrow these too
▶ Food and water for the animal(s)
▶ Camera

What you do:

▶ Establish whether any parents or local smallholders are willing to loan you an animal. Choose a small animal that children will not be intimidated by, that is relatively 'low maintenance' and that will be tolerant of handling by children. Hens and rabbits are ideal.

- ▶ Source secure housing for the animal – most likely, from its owner – and choose a location in your outdoor space that is quiet, sheltered and easily supervised.
- ▶ Talk to children about what the animal's health and wellbeing needs are: how are they similar to children's own? How are they different? What routines can children establish to make sure the animal is properly cared for?
- ▶ Encourage children to invent a back-story for the animal: what is its name? Where does it live? Who are its friends and family? What does it do when it's not at your setting?
- ▶ Offer children a camera to document the animal's stay with you – recording where it goes, what it eats, where it sleeps, etc. Share the story with the animal's owner when he or she comes to collect their animal.

Staying safe:

- ▶ Maintain hygiene procedures around animals, paying particular attention to hand washing with antibacterial handwash.
- ▶ Animals can nip; it's important children learn how to handle animals carefully and respectfully to minimise the risk of nips or scratches. Have a first aid kit nearby to attend to cuts and scratches.
- ▶ Ensure borrowed animals are securely housed, whether they are indoors or out. Ensure foxes or other scavengers can't access the animals' housing.
- ▶ Clear up animal food spillages and faeces at the end of the session.

Other ideas...

- ▶ Make life drawings and clay sculptures of the animal.
- ▶ Read stories about farm animals and compare your borrowed animal's life with those of the fictional animals.
- ▶ Once the animal has returned to its usual home, make a visit to compare its own habitat with the habitat you were able to offer it whilst it visited.
- ▶ Search for evidence of wildlife in your own outdoor space – discuss what the evidence tells you about the animal and its habitat and lifestyle.

Internet search:
caring for hens/rabbits /mice; animals in schools; RSPCA

Bottle babies

Inspired by the book 'The Out-of-Sync Child Has Fun', practitioners at Takoma Park Co-operative Nursery School and Windmill Integrated Primary School have pioneered the re-use of 1-litre and 2-litre drinks bottles, filling them with coloured water and calling them 'bottle babies'. These open ended, loose parts resources are rich in affordances, having no obvious 'use' and yet providing children with unlimited potential for play.

Key skills:
gross and fine motor skills; collaboration; speaking and listening; creative expression; agility

What you need:

▶ Lots of 1-litre and 2-litre clear plastic drinks bottles, with lids
▶ Water and food colouring

What you do:

▶ Transport bottle babies around the setting in dolls' prams, bikes and trikes and in baskets.

▶ Use them for counting, sorting, estimating and matching activities.

▶ Roll them down slides and slopes.

▶ Lay them on the ground to make a very wobbly, tricky pathway to walk over.

▶ Place bottle babies on a sunny windowsill or hang them from a fence, to create sparking translucent effects as sunlight filters through them.

▶ Camouflage them around the play space for a treasure hunt, matching the colour of the water with the surrounding features.

▶ Make boundaries and roadway edges by lying the bottle babies down horizontally.

▶ Include a spoonful of glitter in some of the bottles for sparkly bottle babies.

Staying safe:

▶ Use edible food colouring to colour the water in the bottles; seal the bottles tightly so that water cannot leak out; replenish damaged bottles and change all the bottles every 6 months or so.

▶ Set bottle baby ground rules – no taking the lids off, no throwing them around.

Other ideas...

▶ Place flowers, cones, shells, corks or other natural materials into the bottles before filling them with the coloured water – or fill them completely and miss out the water. Observe which objects sink and which float.

Internet search:
Blogs – Learning for Life; Takoma Park Nursery

Take a line for a walk

Journeys into the unknown have always been an exciting part of childhood, and this activity uses a long rope to suggest a journey or route. It's an open-ended resource and emergent play scenarios will unfold according to children's interests and fascinations. Here are just a few suggestions for adult initiated activities.

Key skills:

agility; story telling; problem solving

What you need:

▶ A long length of rope or thick twine, hosepipe or strips of fabric knotted together

I will need

What you do:

▶ Lay the 'line' out on a grassy area; it could be in a straight line or curving around landscape features such as trees and shrubs. Use the line as a wildlife transect – children crawl along it with magnifiers to get a 'worm's eye view', describing what they see as they progress.

▶ Practice measuring techniques by placing the 'line' onto a hard surface and using rulers, trundle wheels, measuring tapes and hands and feet to estimate the length of the line.

▶ Place a really long 'line' on a route around your outdoor space and use it for solo meditation. Try to create an interesting and lengthy route with features to contemplate. Walk along the line, stopping every few metres to 'leave' a child sitting alongside the line. Once every child has been 'left', go back to the beginning and pick up the children again in order. The walk should be completed in silence, presenting each child with the chance to have a peaceful moment in a busy day.

▶ Collect interesting, unusual or familiar artefacts and place them around the outdoor play space, then link them to one another using the 'line'. Take children for a walk along the line, making up a story as you go and incorporating each object spotted along the route; ask children to suggest story ideas. What happens to the story if you reverse the route?

▶ Coil the 'line' into a huge snail shell shape, or a snake, or a whale.

▶ Create an obstacle course by arranging the 'line' around the outdoor space, over and under features, up in the air, around corners, up steps, etc. Encourage children to think about different ways of moving along the line, using all of their bodies and working out the most effective movements and the quickest route.

▶ Balance along a straight length of rope, laid onto a hard, level surface. Children might like to carry a long stick to help them balance, or use hoops and quoits to do acrobatic tricks along the tightrope!

Staying safe:
▶ Always put ropes, twine or fabric strips away securely at the end of every session; use of these resources should be supervised.
▶ Wash hands thoroughly after activities involving crawling, climbing or picking up mini-beasts.

Other ideas...
▶ Enrich stories such as 'The Lighthouse Keeper's Lunch' by erecting a rope and pulley system across the outdoor play space.
▶ Make simple rope swings by tying a piece of timber or a branch to one end of the rope and securely attaching the other to your play equipment or a tree. The 'seat' should not be more than 30cm from the ground, and you must test the branch or equipment with your own weight to be sure it is safe.

Internet search:
rope activities for children

Urban gymnastics

Parkour is an urban gymnastic sport, which utilises natural and man-made features in the environment as gymnastic equipment. Practitioners move quickly between objects, leaping over them, balancing and swinging, climbing and rebounding as they move. The sport builds confidence, agility and strength and makes an effective and enjoyable physical development activity for young children.

Key skills:

agility; hand-eye co-ordination; problem solving; gross motor skills

What you need:

▶ Just the physical features of the environment you have available – benches, tables, climbing frame, low walls, railings, etc.

▶ Sensible shoes – trainers, sports sandals, plimsolls

▶ First aid kit

What you do:

▶ Discuss the Parkour concept with children – if possible, show a short video clip of 'professional' Parkour practitioners in action – there are plenty of dramatic and awe inspiring clips online.

- ▶ Tour the outdoor space together, evaluating the physical features for their Parkour potential – for example, running along benches, jumping over tyres, bouncing off walls, balancing along railings (with help!), leaping from high places and swinging from branches.
- ▶ Warm up with stretching and jogging exercises; like any aerobic activity, Parkour is very physical and requires a warm up.
- ▶ Devise and practise Parkour movements on individual features of your environment – for example, running towards a wall and bouncing off it with both feet; sprinting across a seat, swinging around a lamppost or pole.
- ▶ Once children are confident in their movements at each feature, bring them together into a series, moving quickly between each obstacle, attempting to speeding up interval runs and working on speed, precision and balance at each feature.
- ▶ Cool down at the end of the session.

Staying safe:

- ▶ Parkour will inevitably involve bumps and scrapes. Be sure parents are aware of your intentions, the risk benefit assessment you've carried out, and the strategies you intend to use to minimise harm.
- ▶ Keep a first aid kit with you at all times and ensure all participants are wearing sensible shoes.
- ▶ Check that objects children are likely to utilise are sturdy and appropriate for very active play.
- ▶ You may need to explain to children that it isn't always appropriate to Parkour through the outdoor space – for example, if features are already being used by other children.

Other ideas...

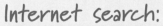

- ▶ Use loose parts play resources to create a Parkour-style obstacle course – for example, incorporating logs, tyres and objects to weave in and out of and items to leap over.
- ▶ Visit a local park, experimenting with Parkour movements on the way there and using the play equipment in ways children have not tried before.

Internet search:
Parkour UK; free running for children

Evaluating your free and found activities

Introducing free and found resources won't be expensive, but it will require time and effort on your part, so it's vital you are able to justify this 'investment'. How will you know that your new treasure trove of free and found materials is having a positive impact on outcomes for your children? In common with the introduction of any new approach or resource, evaluation is crucial, and begins with a clear understanding of your 'starting point'. Knowing 'where you are now' will allow you to later look back and review progress against a set of baseline data and will provide evidence of the need for change.

If you already have a robust planning and evaluation tool, then it makes sense to use it to establish the value of your new resources. Alternatively, the following planning and evaluation cycle might help.

Where are we now?

Audit outdoor play at your setting, examining the elements that combine to enable high quality outdoor play: how the space is managed and resourced; the skills and deployment of the workforce; and the quality of the environment itself. Areas to investigate include:

a.   Where do children like to play – and where do they not? Who are they playing with? What are they playing with?

b.   The quality and condition of the features, fixtures and resources in the play space.

c.   The effect external factors have on the quality of outdoor play – for example, weather, traffic noise, shared use of the space.

d.   The effectiveness and accessibility of storage and the accessibility of the space itself.

e.   The role of the practitioners. How engaged are they? How confident? How playful?

The answers to these questions will paint a picture of overall outdoor provision as it is now, and should highlight gaps and opportunities for improvement.

Setting objectives and planning for change

Review your setting's overall improvement plan; what role could free and found resources outdoors have in meeting these improvement targets?

Focus on two or three really meaningful objectives, making sure they are realistic and likely to be achievable with the introduction of free and found resources. Once you've agreed these objectives, decide how you will know whether they have been met and include a timescale if you can. You could also refer to the early learning goals or experiences and outcomes within your early years curriculum to record how outdoor play resources are supporting improved outcomes for children.

For example, if your audit or setting improvement plan identified 'increasing children's independence' as a priority, you should begin by identifying what the barriers to independence are, then establish how you could use thoughtfully chosen free and found resources to help children become more independent. Resources that encourage children to lead and extend their own play will help, as will storage facilities that pro-vide simple access and play spaces that lend themselves to particular types of play (e.g. active play, collaborative play).

Making the changes and measuring success

As you begin to introduce new free and found play resources, monitor how (and where, and by whom) they are used – remembering that this may not be quite the way you'd anticipated. The rich affordances of open-ended play resources mean that you may discover unexpected outcomes.

As each new free and found resource is introduced, take time to show the items to children, discussing what the objects are, where they have come from and what they might have been used for. Allow children to use their senses to explore the objects and encourage them to think about how to safely use the items outdoors. This is particularly important if children will be using tools or equipment to make the most of the free and found resources.

Remember to evaluate against your initial objectives, and look back at the issues your audit identified right at the start. Being able to demonstrate that small, cost effective interventions have contributed to improvements in the quality of outdoor play will boost everyone's confidence and encourage further development outdoors.

You should also share what you've learned:

▶ Talk to parents about the games and activities that your free and found resources have inspired, and encourage them to take on the free and found challenge in their own homes and gardens.

▶ Collect your ideas, advice and activities into a binder that can be shared with other colleagues – include your risk benefit assessments and photos and comments illustrating how the resources were used.

▶ Let donors of free and found resources know what you did with their gifts – they are more likely to offer donations again in the future if they can see that their unwanted items have been put to good use.

Further research and useful websites

Reading and research

▶ 'Too safe for their own good?: Helping children learn about risk and skills', by Jennie Lindon

▶ Explore more about affordance theory, starting with Tim Gill's thought provoking blog post: http://rethinkingchildhood.com/tag/affordance

▶ Read about pioneering 'free and found' play at the Learning for Life blog: http://tinyurl.com/L4Llooseparts

▶ Check out the amazing low- and no-cost resource ideas at www.creativestarlearning.co.uk

Guidance

▶ Managing risk in play provision: download a pdf from www.playengland.org.uk

▶ Shared vision and values for outdoor play in the early years: http://tinyurl.com/visionvalues

▶ Read the Health and Safety Executive's High Level Statement on play: www.hse.gov.uk/entertainment/childs-play-statement.htm

Organisations

▶ Find your nearest scrap store: www.scrapstoresuk.org

▶ Rotary clubs: www.ribi.org

▶ The Guardian's 'top 10 recycling sites' - http://tinyurl.com/freebiesites

▶ The Money Saving Expert forums have lots of ideas for recycling and freebies: www.moneysavingexpert.com

▶ Outdoor play training and design projects: www.playlearninglife.org.uk

If you have found this book useful you might also like ...

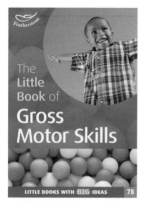

LB Gross Motor Skills
ISBN 978-1-4081-5545-5

LB Making Poetry
ISBN 978-1-4081-1250-2

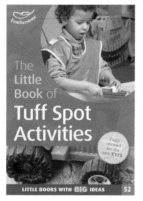

LB Tuff Spot Activities
ISBN 978-1-4729-0733-2

LB Role Play Windows
ISBN 978-1-4081-9506-2

All available from

www.bloomsbury.com/featherstone

The Little Books Club

There is always something in Little Books to help and inspire you. Packed full of lovely ideas, Little Books meet the need for exciting and practical activities that are fun to do, address the Early Learning Goals and can be followed in most settings. Everyone is a winner!

We publish 5 new Little Books a year. Little Books Club members receive each of these 5 books as soon as they are published for a reduced price. The subscription cost is £29.99 – a one off payment that buys the 5 new books for £4.99 instead of £8.99 each.

In addition to this, Little Books Club Members receive:
· Free postage and packing on anything ordered from the Featherstone catalogue
· A 15% discount voucher upon joining which can be used to buy any number of books from the Featherstone catalogue
· Members price of £4.99 on any additional Little Book purchased
· A regular, free newsletter dealing with club news, special offers and aspects of Early Years curriculum and practice
· All new Little Books on approval - return in good condition within 30 days and we'll refund the cost to your club account

Call 020 7758 0200 or email: littlebooks@bloomsbury.com for an enrolment pack. Or download an application form from our website:
www.bloomsbury.com

The **Little Books** series consists of:

- 50
- All through the year
- Bags, Boxes & Trays
- Big Projects
- Bricks & Boxes
- Celebrations
- Christmas
- Circle Time
- Clay and Malleable Materials
- Clothes and Fabric
- Colour, Shape and Number
- Cooking from Stories
- Cooking Together
- Counting
- Dance
- Dance Music CD
- Dens
- Discovery Bottles
- Dough
- Drama from Stories
- Explorations
- Fine Motor Skills
- Free and Found
- Fun on a Shoestring
- Games with Sounds
- Gross Motor Skills
- Growing Things
- ICT
- Investigations
- Junk Music
- Kitchen Stuff
- Language Fun
- Light and Shadow
- Listening
- Living Things
- Look and Listen
- Making Books and Cards
- Making Poetry
- Maps and Plans
- Mark Making
- Maths Activities
- Maths from Stories
- Maths Outdoors
- Maths Problem Solving
- Maths Songs and Games
- Messy Play
- Minibeast Hotels
- Multi-sensory Stories
- Music
- Nursery Rhymes
- Opposites
- Outdoor Play
- Outside in All Weathers
- Painting
- Parachute Play
- Persona Dolls
- Phonics
- Playground Games
- Prop Boxes for Role Play
- Props for Writing
- Puppet Making
- Puppets in Stories
- Resistant Materials
- Rhythm and Raps
- Role Play
- Role Play Windows
- Sand and Water
- Science through Art
- Scissor Skills
- Seasons
- Sequencing Skills
- Sewing and Weaving
- Small World Play
- Sound Ideas
- Special Days
- Stories from around the world
- Story bags
- Storyboards
- Storybuilding
- Storytelling
- Time and Money
- Time and Place
- Topsy Turvy
- Traditional Tales
- Treasure Baskets
- Treasure Boxes
- Tuff Spot Activities
- Washing lines
- Woodwork
- Writing

All available from
www.bloomsbury.com